MW01256953

You're Doing Just Fine

Prose & Poetry

from a past that was never present

Charlotte Eriksson

The Glass Child

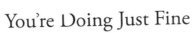

You're Doing Just Fine
prose & poetry from a past that was never present
***

Discography
Charlotte Eriksson EP, 2011
This Is How Ghosts Are Made EP, 2011
Songs of An Insomniac EP, 2011
I'd Like To Remain A Mystery, LP 2013
Empty Roads & Broken Bottles: in search for The Great Perhaps, book 2013
Love Always, Your Tragedy EP, 2013
I Must Be Gone and Live, or Stay and Die, LP 2014
Another Vagabond Lost To Love, book 2015
You're Doing Just Fine, book 2015
Under Northern Skies, LP 2016
This Silence Now, EP 2017
Coming Home, EP 2017
Everything Changed When I Forgave Myself, book 2018
Feeling Everything, Holding on to Nothing, LP 2021
He loved me some days. I'm sure he did., book 2021

This book is meant to be read little by little, page by page,
like small reminders of hope, of belonging,
of telling you
that you
are not alone.

There is a new day every day, and
happiness is not a place. It's moment by moment, breath by breath,
and you
are not wrong or far off track
but right in time.
Doing the right thing, in the right way,
at the right time.
It's during the hard days we grow our strength.

You matter.

Love always
Charlotte

YOU'RE DOING JUST FINE

Take a shower. Wash away every trace of yesterday. Of smells. Of weary skin. Get dressed. Make coffee. Windows open, the sun shining through. Hold the cup with two hands and notice that you feel the feeling of warmth.

You still feel warmth.

Now sit down and get to work. Keep your mind sharp, head on, eyes on the page and if small thoughts of worries fight their ways into your consciousness: throw them off like fires in the night and keep your eyes on the track. Nothing but the task in front of you.

Get off your chair in the middle of the day. Put on your shoes and take a long walk on open streets around people. Notice how they're all walking, in a hurry, or slowly. Smiling, laughing, or eyes straight forward, determined to get to wherever they're going. And notice how you're just one of them. Not more, not less. Find comfort in the way you're just one in the crowd. Your worries: no more, no less.

Go back home. Take the long way just to not pass the liquor store. Don't buy the cigarettes. Go straight home. Take off your shoes. Wash your hands. Your face. Notice the silence. Notice your heart. It's still beating. Still fighting. Now get back to work.

Work with your mind sharp and eyes focused and if any thoughts of worries or hate or sadness creep their ways around, shake them off like a runner in the night for you own your mind, and you need to tame it. Focus. Keep it sharp on track, nothing but the task in front of you. Work until your eyes are tired and head is heavy, and keep working even after that.

Then take a shower, wash off the day. Drink a glass of water. Make the room dark. Lie down and close your eyes. Notice the silence. Notice your heart. Still beating. Still fighting.

You made it, after all. You made it, another day. And you can make it one more.

You're doing just fine.

You're doing just fine.

Under Love's Heavy Burden Do I Sink

— Shakespeare, Romeo & Juliet

YESTERDAY

It could be yesterday,
when I was less in love,
I think,
for I did not see you in the mirror
behind me
while getting dressed.
The way your hands couldn't stay away
and our bodies always found their ways back to each other,
as if they were meant to be together,
close.

But then it was today and I saw you
again
in the mirror,
behind me while getting dressed.

So I go to sleep tonight,
alone,
without actually falling asleep, scared of the moment I will wake up
and realize it was just a dream.
You're really gone.

Now all I can do is get through to another tomorrow,
hoping that I will be less in love
again,
like yesterday.
But not
today.

PLAY PRETEND

Can we stay, just a little, still some rum in the bottle,
I always get my way.
There was a fire on the other side of the water and it lit up the sky like
nothing was ordinary.

Okay, I go first: tell me about the way people matter to people but
never enough to not be fooled
by human urges
like me.
It's a game I play like *1 - 2 - 3:*
let's see how the people they should care about the most
hardly matter at all
and it's a lose/lose situation.
I'm the spark from the last second of a fallen star,
exciting at times but then there's the fade,
the vague memory left and nothing to keep
or store
and I'm back to hiding my own shadow, trying not to be too real.
Back, back, reality check,
They snap their fingers like 'wake me up' and
I'm sorry for the escapism. I'm sorry for your mistake.

Call me a myth, call me the imagined.
I can take it, love, just make it loud. Make it echo
like every word does in between my ribcage
and I will swallow it whole every night on my own
with new strangers and new comets
but I can take it.
Lay it all on me and watch me carry it like a soldier
without a sword

as I vagabond my way to find new lovers to fool
and kiss
and say goodbye
it's just a game I play like *1 - 2 - 3:*
let's see how much the people they say they love the most
hardly matter at all.

MEDITATION ON SILENCE

Sometimes you need to sit lonely on the floor in a quiet room in order to hear your own voice and not let it drown in the noise of others.

xx   xxx x

I found myself sitting lonely on the floor in a quiet room and realized that all these voices in my head, screaming 'yes' and 'no' and 'do not rest,' are not my own. Sometimes you run and work and laugh and fight, for the chase, maybe, or for the simple reason that out there in the crowd, around the people, you can drown out the heaviness and make sure there is no time left to doubt and so you just go go go!

But then you find yourself sitting lonely on the floor in a quiet room, and all these voices you've lived with for so long around the people are gone, and you're left with only you and your own and there is nowhere to run or hide. You've got to face the truth. Your own truth. Your own voice. Which is quiet, calm, scared even, because it hasn't gotten the chance to speak up lately, for it was drowned out by all the other voices saying 'yes' and 'no' and 'do not rest' but now there are no more masks. No more walls.

Sometimes you need to sit lonely on the floor in a quiet room and just listen. Listen to your own voice without trying to change it, please it, lead it—just listen. It is easy to know who you are when you're inventing a character; it is harder to find out who you are without inventing it.

I GO TO THE OCEAN TO SAY GOODBYE

The stars are brilliant at this time of night.
I wander these streets like a ritual I don't dare to break,
 and it's quite glorious.

I left him by the water's edge,
still waving long after the ship was gone,
and if someone would have screamed my name I wouldn't have heard
for I've said goodbye so many times in my short and strange life that
farewells are a muscular task and I've taught mine well.
There's a place by the side of the railway near the lake where I grew up
and I used to go there to bury things and start anew.
    I used to go there to say goodbye.
I was young and did not know many people but I had hidden things
inside me that I never dared to show and in silence I tried to kill them,
one way or the other,
leaving sin on my body,
scrubbing tears off with salt,
and I built my rituals in farewells.
Endings I still cling to.

So I go to the ocean to say goodbye.

He left that morning, the last words still echoing in my head,
and though he said he'll come back one day I know a broken promise
from a right one
for I have used them myself and there is no coming back.
Minds like ours can't be tamed and the price for freedom is the price
we pay.

I turned away from the ocean

as not to fall for its plea,
for it used to seduce and consume me,
and there was this one night
a few years back when I was not yet accustomed to farewells,
and just like now I stood waving long after the ship was gone.
But I was younger then and easily fooled
and the ocean was deep and dark and blue
and I took my shoes off to let the water freeze my bones.
I waded until I could no longer walk and it was too cold to swim but
still I kept on walking at the bottom of the sea for I could not tell the
difference between the ocean and the lack of someone I loved and I
had not yet learned how the task of moving on is a muscular task,
a skill you need to learn,
as necessary as survival.

Days passed by and I spent them with my work.
And now I'm writing letters I will never dare to send
but even so I write them, for maybe one day our paths will cross and
then I will be ready for clean slates and new beginnings.
For there is this one day every year or so,
when the burden gets too heavy,
and I collect my belongings I no longer need,
and I make my way to the ocean to burn and drown and start anew,
and it's quite wonderful, setting flames on written words.
I stand there, staring deep into the fire until they're all gone
and I'm ready to move on. Nothing left to hold me back.

You kissed me that morning as if you'd never done it before and never
would again and now I write another letter that I will never dare to
send, collecting memories of loss like chains tight around my chest,
and if you see a fire from the shore tonight
it's my chains going up in flames.

JOURNAL I

We counted days in coffee pots, like it took us two hours to finally close our eyes after we said goodnight, and even then did we not sleep. Wrapped in white sheets and big open windows, sun leaking in to wake us up. I was unbearably happy, and so were you, and that's why it didn't last. You need the balance and we had none. Two flyers jumping straight out with no thought of a parachute and that's why we flew too beautifully and recklessly
and that's why it crushed us
  brutally
when we hit the ground.

SMOKE LIKE FOG

May. Budweiser. Smoke like fog.
He said goodbye this morning,
I held him tight until he said "just go,"
so there I went
and I am still sorry.

I took him to the river and said "let's watch something drown,"
So he took a stone
and I took my necklace
and we threw it all together,
the way I always think I will get better in July.
Things will change and sounds won't ache
and I gave my heart to uncertainty so many times,
so I took him to the river,
threw the necklace into the river to slowly watch it drown,
or burn, or fade away
like I've done so many times.

Now it's summer and it's youth, like road trips going out to nowhere,
and it's an easy ride when you don't want much,
but I do want
much
and there are things that won't get me there.
Like May, Budweiser, smoke like fog.
Feeling sorry or throwing memories in rivers,
like love thrown out at sea.

So it's summer. So it's youth,
and I'm back on my way going out to nowhere

by myself
for that's where I belong
and one day it might lead me somewhere
new
and that's where I'll go.

He left this morning, away to where I'm not.
I held on tight until he said "just go"
and there I went
and so it goes.

So it always fucking goes.

DEJA VU

I'm sorry I left.
I'm sorry I'm drinking.
I'm sorry I can't tell you more.

"He wanted all to lie in an ecstasy of peace; I wanted all to sparkle and dance in a glorious jubilee. I said his heaven would be only half alive; and he said mine would be drunk: I said I should fall asleep in his; and he said he could not breathe in mine."

— Emily Brontë, *Wuthering Heights*

MIND / MATTER

The lions surpassed me though I ran with all I had. I've been clinging
to the darkness, not letting my skin face the light
or other people
for I might look pretty from time to time from a distance
or a glance
but see, all I ever wanted was to look like I felt
or feel the way I looked
for they never matched up. Always making turns and pushing down
and then there was my mind, in between it all, never choosing side.

I tried to change my outer to look like I felt,
for I never spoke much about the things that really mattered, to me,
still making up my mind about what that really is. I value people and
those who stay around and I wouldn't want to waste the time I have
with them, for time is rare, for people like me, with people like them.
Laughing is empty unless someone replies, and so I wouldn't want to
waste it by telling tales about inner matching outer
so you will mostly hear me laugh. Mostly hear me sing and joke and
smile
and drink and smoke and run
but those are details for people like them
so you will mostly hear me laugh.

My outer changed and looked as rotten as my insides,
as empty as my heart and unnourished as my soul
and I opened doors screaming
"can't you see it now?! Can't you hear it now?!"
but then people looked with disgust,
sometimes worry,
sometimes not.
Sticking close to the ground,

averting their eyes,
and so there I stood.
Looking as rotten as I was inside,
scratching marks off my skin.

I switched my plan, valued mind over matter and stuck to my roots.
Poisoned my inner instead of my outer, to grow rotten from inside out
instead
I thought.
Because these are the times I live in, I argued, where my inner can stay
ugly as long as my outer stay clean and no one will ever argue or
question or hear
or see
or ask
beyond more than what they see
so there I went.
Setting fire to myself as the others go to bed
and now I'm throwing caution in the wind as I race with the lions,
watching sunrise after sunrise from different altered states of mind
and as long as I keep clean on the outside
my insides can stay rotten
like I feel
for they never matched up anyway
and what's a youth to do. With all these days
and nights
and freedom of choice
to do whatever I please,
whatever I choose.

The lions surpassed me
and I surrender to their ropes.

They chase for the sake of the chase
as I do too
for I have nothing to win or gain or keep
or lose
so I run with the lions,
 throwing myself into the ring.

The lions surpassed me
and I surrender to their ropes.

THE ROOM

I sit in a room made up of four walls and no window,
catching glances of myself from above.
But I am not there —
I'm here, on the floor,
arms wrapped tight around myself,
to comfort
or shelter.
I am sitting lonely in a room made up of four walls and no window.

It was a beautiful sunset,
the rare ones you only get during August
and sometimes in the spring
when the whole sky turns pink and purple
and all sorts of free
and we stood there
on a bridge where I don't live
but would like to
because I've been glorifying the starting over of my whole damned life
and I still am and probably always will be
for there is something in the beating of my heart
when I realize that this is not it. This is not final
or permanent
and you can start anew at any given moment.
Do whatever you please
or maybe don't please, right now,
but maybe you could grow to like it, because life is just the passage of
time and it's up to you to pass it as you please.

...
I am sitting lonely in an empty room with four walls and no window. The
shadows are dancing wild, though I don't know how because there's no

light to make them come alive but still there they are
and who are you to tell me it's all in my head? And how am I to know if
your vision is more real than mine
because I know for sure that I see the shadows
dancing wild on the walls
but I also know for sure
that nothing grows without the light from the window
and so who am I to trust?

Let me tell you a story:
I was once declared disordered. Mentally unstable, they said, and I
shrugged my shoulders and kept on walking, for it didn't mean a thing
to me, like it did for them, and what was I supposed to make of it?
So on I went, unstable as I was, and there were nights when I saw
shadows on my walls and no one else did, but still I welcomed them
and admired them. Observed with clarity so clear you only get from
not being
really clear
and that's all I can say for now.

These are days of confessions
I've noticed
and if the lack of confessions is what stands in the way of staying and
moving on, then I am not scared.
To say this or that for if that's what it takes to free myself
this time, *from time,*
then I will throw confessions like raptures in the storm for I've been
running in the dark
too deep and too far and lonely
lately and I remember days when all felt light.
I felt light and kind and fine.

....

I am sitting lonely on the floor in an empty room
and sometimes that's what it takes to let go of expectations of what to
see and what to feel
for when no one is watching, or telling me what to see, I can see what
I actually see, and more often than not that does not match up. So you
can call me unstable. Call me mental and disturbed. I am aware of the
way my weaknesses are growing into possibilities
like I've trained them to
and if speaking up is what it takes to free myself
then that is what I will be doing because I know that I'm not alone
and that is why I write.
I know that I am not alone
and this is why I write.

I am sitting lonely in an empty room and I see things that others don't
and that's why I write. So the question is not if you can change what I
see, but if you will let me write
so I can let you know
that you are not alone
either.

(If you see shadows on the walls
that no one else sees,
you are not alone)

YOU ARE NOT AN APOLOGY

Never apologize for how you live your life,
or not live your life.
Never apologize for your loneliness
or stubbornness
or will to survive,
and never soak in the words of someone who in any way belittles you.

People put other people down because they themselves are not certain
enough
if they, in fact,
are standing themselves.

YOU ARE NOT ALONE

I don't really want to be doing this and if I could stop writing this very second I would.

It started like this:
I was the kid with a grey hoodie slamming the door at midnight. My mandatory seat in class was near the entrance because I was always late and it took four months for my classmates to learn my name.
I was the kid climbing up the roof to smoke the mess away and I was the one who never wanted to come down. There are all sorts of ways to study and I never found the answers in the system of 9-5 with grades, and it never did me any good either
because what made me open my eyes every morning to the sound of heavy rain against the concrete was not the thought of a future with grades or scholarships, reputations and educations; exceptional behavior to fit my salary.

I was the kid with a grey hoodie slamming the door at midnight to walk on empty streets until the sun woke up,
and I was not alone.
I spent my days so god damn lonely around those constant talking people, but at night, as I walked on empty streets, I was not alone. I walked with the heroes of my world. With the writers and singers and talkers and thinkers and I got them. I understood them and I had the same song on repeat for nights on end because each note he took assured me that I was not alone. Someone out there knew and understood and got it and that was enough to keep those legs walking, keep this voice training, keep my fingers typing, because one day, maybe one day, if I learned how to write clear enough, sing loud enough, be strong enough, I could explain myself in a way that made

sense and then maybe one day, one day, someone out there would hear
and recognize and I could let them know that they are not alone. Just
like that song I had on repeat for several nights, as I walked lonely on
empty streets, let me know that I was not
alone,
and that's how it starts.

So there are days I don't want to be doing this.
The knife is beautifully sharp and my room is clean, the bottles
emptied and I have nothing left to give.
But then a clear spark from the edge of the knife, and I realize that
someone out there might feel exactly what I feel this very damned
second
and she might hold that knife
on the floor in the corner
pressed closed to the wall
and in the flicker of an eye I throw the gun down and hide the knife
and run to type this because I need you to know that
you
are
not
alone
and I'm still practicing hard to learn these words
and I spend my nights rearranging them, decorating them
to maybe one day write well enough to make sense of myself
and sing loud enough to explain
myself
but for what it's worth with this messy way of language I'm holding
today
YOU
ARE
NOT

ALONE.

When the others were picked up and walked home by friends or
fathers or best friend's sisters,
I was the kid in a grey hoodie, walking with the poets, the singers, the
thinkers, and I was not alone.

JOURNAL II

I dreamt about us for months after you were gone. Where we would be, who we would be, what we would do if you still would be here. But you're not, here, so I hold tight to the illusion of what could have been. Sometimes it feels more real than what real ever could be, and sometimes I think that's all I'll ever have.

Illusions of what could be.

Illusions of what we could be.

Illusions
of what could be.

DRUNK ON SOMEONE ELSE'S LOVE

5am
again,
drunk on someone else's love,
or couch,
and I've never felt more at home.

I fled myself,
from the life I've built
because I've been inhabiting routines I don't want to stand for.
Inhabiting skin I'd rather shed
but still took on
like a soldier serving his country,
for that's what they told me to do.
But I was not
strong
or wise,
but young and foolish,
for what is this thing? Trading passions for a tiny bit of acceptance,
and I am not a Sunday morning inside four walls
with clean blood
and organized drawers.
I am the hurricane setting fire to the forests
at night when no one else is alive,
or awake,
however you choose to see it,
and I live in my own flames.
Sometimes burning too bright and too wild
to make things last
or handle
myself or anyone else

30

and so I run.
Run run run,
far and wide
until my bones ache and lungs split
and it feels good.
Hear that, people? It feels good,
because I am the slave and ruler of my own body
and I wish to do with it exactly as I please,
and living in this skin is hard and painful, most of the times, because I
never volunteered to take this on. The daily sacrifice of heart over
mind,
the forever ongoing task of explaining this and that,
and why I don't want to look like this and
be like that
but still here I am and if this is the body I've been given I'm sure as
hell gonna make it work.
If this is the place I've been given, I'm sure as hell gonna make this
work.

So I fled the me that was never really me and I'm on my way.
To newer lands and uncleaned streets
for I've had enough of childish safety in comfort.
Enough of all telling me to look and do, like this and that,
and I never meant to please anyone but myself
and you can call me selfish,
throw words like knives in the dark
but I will not listen,
for not listening to sharp words
brought me to where I am today
and I believe in the path I've been given.
If my only task in this life is to walk it,
I surely will walk it

prouder than anyone else.

If this is the path I've been given,
I will walk it
prouder than anyone else,
for no one else can.

I AM NOT A BROKEN HEART

I am not a broken heart.
I am not collarbones or drunken letters never sent. I am not the way I
leave or left or didn't know how to handle anything
at any time,
and I am not your fault.

I found a small spark by the end of the tunnel I built around us and I
ran as fast as I could with the breath in my throat, scared like hell to
lose sight of the only light I'd seen
since you
left.

You were the hardest year of my life and I've never been so happy.
What does that say about me?

I was never afraid of the dark and I spent my youth walking through
empty playgrounds at midnight, worried mothers telling girls to be
careful and "the world is an ugly place and not everyone wants you
well". But I was not afraid, and I wished for adrenaline to make my
veins pulsate in that way that puts them more on the outside of my
skin than inside.
After the first night with you I never walked alone at night again
because suddenly I had something to lose. Something to save.

I am slowly trying hard to blur out the last months because they're
ugly and I don't want us to be the evidence of how easy it is for heaven
to turn into hell
so I try to recall the beginning.
The early mornings waking up before dawn. The pink sky and the way
you loved the view of the rooftops while the world was still asleep. Or
when we were too far apart for even a day and so the text waking me

33

up, every day a floaty thing I never wanted to leave and I was not worried.

I lied, which I often do, because the truth is a privilege you never earned and you turned cold and unkind and I just wanted to do you well.
Because I've never done anyone well before
or cared about anyone being well
in the same way I cared about you.
I just wanted to do you well even though you never did me well.
I lied. I hate who I became when I was with you.

So I am not a broken heart.
I am not the weight I lost or miles I ran and I am not the way I slept on my doorstep under the bare sky in smell of tears and whiskey because my apartment was empty and if I were to be this empty I wanted something solid to sleep on. Like concrete.
I am not this year and I am not your fault.
I am muscles building cells, a little every day, because they broke that day.
But bones are stronger once they heal and I am smiling to the bus driver again, replacing my groceries once a week and I am not sitting for hours in the shower anymore.
I am the way a life unfolds and blooms and seasons come and go and I am the way the spring always finds a way to turn even the coldest winter into a field of green and flowers and new life.
I am not your fault.

ON LONELINESS

"But you're lonely,"
he said, as a question turned out as a statement, glancing at me, as if to
say he's sorry but still never really meant it. Maybe so, I thought, or
said, and kept my eyes on the moon.
It's May, like youth, and the nights in Berlin are warm, made for
never-ending. We missed the last bus, like we always do, and walked
slowly in no hurry. He's got nice hands to hold and those are rare these
days, like a reminder of not being lonely, even though he says I am
and I say 'maybe so' and keep my mind on the moon.

So let's talk about my loneliness.
I need the city and I need the lack of it. I need silence and I need the
crowd, for I live in my head most of the time, staying up until my
friendly neighbor next-door leaves for work and I watch him stumble
off, from my window, where I sit. I live as much as I can and people
are a rarity I never get enough of, but still—still—all I want to do is
write. Create. Nothingness turned into something and I can shape my
own self and ways, design and recreate and people will believe, if I tell
it well enough. I am not a poem, but I aspire to be one.
I'm possessed and obsessed with words and worlds and these
possibilities I see in the spaces in between. Maybe it's the way it took
me half a lifetime to discover and learn, this, the shaping of words, but
the day I did is still visioned clear in my head, and I am still a child,
sitting wide-eyed in the middle of the night, it's like ecstasy, the way I
place these lines, here and there, rhythms to shape and rhymes to
recreate. My fingers fly like in hypnosis and I don't know how it
happens or where it comes from but suddenly
I wake up
and sit up
and there it is.

The evidence of the last minute, hour, week—year—and I'm free.
Nothingness turned into something. Me—I, turned into someone.
Someone I wish to be.

See, writing is about freeing yourself (freeing myself) from hidden
burdens,
for I bottle up opinions and experiences, emotions and values,
and no one gets close enough here
and so I run home after every encounter to bleed it out.
Some things need to be whispered, like a slow hymn on a worn-out
guitar. Other things need to be screamed and belted from a stage with
no endings, and other things should be kept written, read, and never
to be spoken out loud. "Choose your craft," they tell me, as if I can't
be more than one thing, please more than one crowd. But see, my
favorite pieces of art are magical realism for who are you or them or I
to say that nothing isn't good enough and some things should just be
taken as they are.
Like me,
and my loneliness,
admired holiness,
for it teaches me.

It was a peaceful night and we wandered by ourselves but still together
and he kept saying "but you're lonely" and after a few "maybe so"s he
just smiled and took my hand and so did I and it was nice. It's all in
the silence, the moments in between the noise and conversations I
value the most, for that's where things grow. Like stillness after a
hurricane, when you take a breath and say "damn, what a night." Or
like
loneliness
after a long time of being known,

and you come home to your empty room and lie on the floor and say
"so many words saying nothing at all."

"You're lonely," they say,
but it doesn't scare me
anymore
for it teaches me,
and maybe that's the biggest win from these years:
I don't need anyone else to distract me from myself anymore,
like I always thought I would.
I don't break mirrors anymore,
like I always thought I would.

I can finally stand myself,
and I never thought I would.

DON'T BE SCARED. GO. LOVE.

You will meet someone who will give a new definition to your name. Like it suddenly means the whole universe and has room for every kind of flower there is, and he says it like it was always meant to sound like that. Things that always have annoyed you in people suddenly turn into the most hypnotizing habits when they come from him, and it's all exactly as it's supposed to be. He will make you forget about all the things you used to strive for, wonder and regret, and he will build a new world up, in your head, where no one else lives. He'll hold your hand and every glance feels like a thousand words and you will not worry.

You will dig up all those old poems and books about love and hope that you never understood, but now you do and it's all so wonderful! You will be kissed in every possible way and you will love and be loved and there will be a small tiny voice in your head whispering that nothing lasts forever but you will not listen. You will shut it out and go on loving because what else is there to do.

But then the days pass by and summer leaves for winter and as the mornings stay darker for longer and longer you will sense an unbalance. A shift in the atmosphere, and his hands a little colder, his voice a little stronger.

The winter will come and you will wake up one day and tell yourself that you are not in love, anymore. You will slow it down, scale it, fight with every fibre of your being to not be the one left alone. To not be the one who stays when it's time to leave and you are determined to not love him, anymore. But the heart was never good with orders and you can't stop something you never meant to start in the first place because it's all in the way forces make the heart want what it wants, no matter how old the sayings are – they have survived for a reason.

I will leave the catastrophe blank for you to fill, and instead tell you
that it will get better,
in a while,
and you will be well again, though you can't see it now,
and you will travel again and eat again and your muscles will grow
stronger, again. You will run and laugh and sing and one day you will
meet someone who makes your heart beat with no pattern again,
and you might try to hide or protect yourself, or compare the different
states of love,
but you must not grow up, must not act wise
  when it comes to love.
You must stay foolish and fall
for every heart will beat in different ways together with yours and love
is not meant to be compared, only enjoyed, and suffered, and
remembered.

So you will meet many 'someones' who will give a new definition to
your name. And you can not build walls, must not close the door, and
please don't hide,
because if you ask me about hurt
  and love
I will say love. Love because the hurt will come and go no matter
what, but only love makes it worthwhile. Only love can cure it.
  Don't be scared. Go. Love.

DEAR ME,

ONE DAY I'LL MAKE YOU PROUD

HANG ON. YOU WILL BE OK.

You can get yourself a small room in a new city
where no one knows your name
just yet
but they will,
for they will see you walk quietly through the market
on Sunday mornings,
and sitting at the cafe on Tuesdays
scribbling thoughts in that worn-out notebook,
or in the library between the shelves of different worlds,
and late on Friday evenings
you will sit peacefully in the corner of the pub
by yourself
and you will be okay with that.
Some nights beautiful boys will buy you drinks
and ask your name
and you will smile, but be okay with walking home
alone
because one day someone will know you
without asking your name
and that's the person that matters.

So wait a few years,
until you can get yourself a small room in a new city
where no one knows your name
just yet
but they will
and there will be an older lady
knocking at your door
saying hi and you're very welcome,
and you can have a garden

where only flowers grow, with no thorns,
that you plant yourself,
and on sunny mornings in April
you can sit and watch them bloom
a little more each day,
just like you do,
bloom a little more
each day.
And on crisp winter mornings in January
you can drink coffee in the cold
on your own front porch
and the town is empty
but full
of other things
like space.
And hope.
And purity.

Wait a few years,
when things are clearer,
and you will go on well.
Just hold on
and wait.

You will be okay.

PRAGUE

August, 2014.

I told my therapist about him and them and all the rest
and he told me to go away for a while
and I would never argue with someone who makes his living listening
to people like me,
singing stories like elegies,
and so I did.
I've gone away.

It's this thing I do, ever so often, since that year, that winter, that thing
that happened,
and now I need to stick to myself
and so I go away.

It's this thing I do, ever so often, to remind myself of the fact that
I
am
okay.
I am okay on my own by myself and I no longer depend on anyone or
anything to be simply
okay,
and that's all I've ever asked for.
I just want to go on well.

It's been a long year and I've met more people than I'm used to
because I used to be fine in my loneliness,
but something,
or someone,
snapped me out of it.
Showed me company. What it's like to feel like home.

and so the going on by myself part wasn't as easy anymore.
But seasons happened and things got colder and harder and suddenly I
found myself smoking circles in the air
by myself in the snow
and I was not okay.

So now it's this thing I do.
I go away, ever so often, by myself, for myself,
to new places with foreign streets I haven't walked yet,
and there I wander, up and down, watching people going places I
don't know
and it always hits me that they're never alone,
always with someone,
and I wonder how they would spend a day all on their own in a
foreign city with nothing to do and no one to see,
and I wonder if they'd be happy.
Just simply being free,
like I am trying to be.
Happy.
Just simply being me.

There are people I think of
more often than not
and there's been one person I've thought of
more often than not
lately
and the hard part is not needing someone,
looking up to someone,
desiring someone,
but being with someone and still staying me,
as the person I've grown to be,
and that's why I need to leave from time to time

to remind myself that I am free
and me
and fine with that.

I am me,
and I just want to be fine with that.

MY WORLD COLLAPSES INTO FICTION

Taking the long way home. Changing the tube a few times extra, even though I don't have to. I spend hours at the café, observing how they talk. How they move, drink, laugh and sound. They speak a strange language I don't understand and I don't wish to make sense of it, or this place, because I never saw the beauty in logic and I wish to keep things sacred, my own, the way I wish it to be.

This is the destruction of habits, the sacrifice of routines
and my world collapses into fiction because I can create these people I'm surrounded by in any way I want. I imagine what they might be talking about, who they might be, and what they might want to get out of this, and that, and life – and I don't wish to know the truth.
It's the way a simple coffee in the morning can turn into the most amazing conversation with a traveling boy from Australia, talking about the simple pleasures of this strange and marvelous world, like kangaroos and the way he pronounced cappuccino. It's the way I got lost while running last night and ended up by a small, quiet lake outside of town. How I sat down while the sun made its way behind the trees and realized that sometimes silence is louder than noise. I let my head rest on the bare cliff, feeling the sun refuel every bone of this strange body I've been given, and I'm still not very friendly with myself at all times, but I'm trying.
It's the way I let go of my personal history when I dedicate myself to the journeying, the wandering, and that's one step closer to becoming accustomed to my own self. To who I've grown to be and wish to be, not who I've been or thought I was.
It's the way it's easier to get to know people when they don't know your name, and they don't care, because it's all about the here and now and the next word and this very place. Sharing a coffee, a beer, a conversation at 2am on the bus back to the hostel. It's the way I wake

up in cheap rented rooms with no air conditioning, one bag of belongings and my guitar and it's all I ever asked for because I have the whole world for myself. No destination, because this journey is the destination, and I don't wish to end up anywhere.

So it's the small things. The way everything can change with each step on these foreign streets, like every second is the discovery of something new I didn't know before. And it doesn't have to be magnificent for others, as long as it's marvelous through my eyes, in my memory. Like waking up at dawn before the sunrise to make my way to the highest place I can find in this town, and then observe how it comes alive. Just watching, sitting, being. And then tell about it. Sing about it. Capture, re-shape, remember.

I might not be where I thought I would be by now, but I wouldn't change a thing, because I still am,
and that's more than I ever thought I would be by now.

THE BOY

I don't want to be this lonely
I always think
as I walk away.

This is what happened:
I was sitting in the corner of the coffee shop where I always sit this
time of day, and I never notice the people because I'm not in their
world, but in mine. Walls of words and characters and letters never
sent
but today it was different, because there was a boy with brown eyes
and no smile and he came in lonely just like I did and he didn't seem
to notice me
or anyone else
and no one seemed to notice him either.
I watched him place his order, say thanks with no heart and not look
up on his way to the table on the other side of the room
where I sat,
observing the boy with brown eyes and no smile.

I don't want to be this lonely
I always think,
and I've never wanted anything more than I wanted to go up to that
boy
with brown eyes
and no smile
and just sit there.
Just let him keep reading
and I could keep writing
and now and then we could look up and give each other a thought,
    because I think he could have beautiful thoughts,

and we could just let each other be less lonely in our loneliness.

But of course I did nothing
and said nothing
and we stayed like that for hours until he finished his book and I had
finished my third coffee and he stood up to leave
and I did not
so I watched him walk away
with no smile
and it was quite a sad view,
or thought,
to know or wonder what might have been.
But that's always the case
with me.
What might have been,
if I wasn't so god damn lonely and stubborn and could move out of
my own way.

I still think about the boy with brown eyes and no smile
and as I sit in the corner of the coffee shop tomorrow I will look up
from time to time when I hear the door open, just in case it's him. Just
in case the boy with brown eyes and no smile would come back and I
would tell him nothing and he would tell me nothing but I think it
would be enough to know that he came back because people rarely do
and I would like to think him different.

I don't want to be this lonely
I always think
and walk away.

IF I STAY

I woke up to a pink sky and the air was crisp and real,
and it was quite a beautiful thing, the way I turned my head and there
you were. Breathing in and out, like nothing could go wrong,
and it was quite a beautiful thing, the way we simply just came to be,
with no effort or trying and slowly we found each other's hands in the
dark. No chains or promises, just a simple sign of hope
that things will go on and get better
and that people and views are still out there, yet to be found
and there you were. Breathing in and out, eyes gently shut, as I woke
up just in time to face the dawn
and it was quite a sad thing,
the way I watched you sleep like nothing could go wrong and I did
not want to harm it, I did not want to blur it, but how could I not
when everything I've ever known has slowly gone away
and I know by now that that's the way you let the new day in
with new roads and views and chances to grow
but it was quite a sad thing
because I don't want this to ever become 'then' or 'was'
and it was quite an unfamiliar thing. The way I took off my shoes
again, put down my bag and quietly went back to bed, slowly between
the sheets of moments I don't want to leave
and it was quite a beautiful thing, the way you had no idea but still
must have known because you did not even open your eyes, but
turned around and took my hand and you were still asleep, breathing
in and out like nothing could go wrong, but still held my hand like
you were glad I didn't leave. 'Thank you for staying',
and it was quite a wonderful thing, the way I smiled and so did you,
sound asleep, and that's all I need to know for now.
That's all I want to know for now.

FEAR IS THE THING

THAT MAKES THE HEART GROW

But if your heart doesn't have any fear
it will cease to grow
in time
for fear is the thing, dear.
Fear is the thing that makes the heart pump,
eyes open and
mind swell,
and fear makes the safety worth chasing.
Adventure awaits on the other side of that fall,
in that fall,
and if you knew the outcome
of each and every thing
the point would cease to be.

Fear is the thing my dear.
Fear is the thing
that makes the heart grow.

CONTRADICTIONS

I can hold my breath
for almost a minute
and I'm practicing to be still
not think
because knowing you makes my mind run wild.

I don't know how to tell you how much I want you.
I've searched for words but words lack consistency
and I've tried to show you
but my hands shake and my eyes flicker
and I've used my body for things out of mind
so nothing matches up.

You touch my shoulder and my spine trembles.
I calm my nerves with another glass
and your breathing is calm,
head slightly tilted,
looking at me like you can't understand
and my blood is out of control.

I can't sleep alone anymore
and I get used to
company
too quickly.
You're always gone too soon.

I have tried to tell you how much I love
the mere thought of you
but my ways go wrong
and my 'love you's turned into apologies

for things I never meant
to say
for kindness turns into anger
and ugly words slip from my mouth
when hearts are pushed into corners
like who the hell are you to steal my breath like this
and heart like that
and I wish I didn't need you
as much as you don't
need me
and I'm sorry.
Dear god I'm sorry
for everything
that didn't confirm
what I wanted to tell you
or show you
as simple as
1, 2, 3 –

it's you
I want
and always will.

INNOCENCE

There's nothing sadder than the ticking beat of a clock in an empty
room.
The keys marching like soldiers with no hesitation.
Complete conformity
and no compassion for the things it causes,
the choices it forces.

I never feel less lonely than when I'm sitting alone on an empty bus,
on an empty road,
just in time to witness the sun rise.
Somewhere far away
where that road ends
or begins
or however you choose to live.
The still sound from the engines
doing their job without my attention,
and the way I get somewhere without fighting.

Taxi drivers are the heroes of our time.
Or at least the heroes of our youth,
or maybe the drunks,
whatever you choose to call me.
It was an awful night with noise and mess
and the chaos that some people cause in my mind
makes me leave before I should,
running barefoot through the entrance.
I had a white dress on and I never wear dresses
but I liked the way it made me feel.
I looked holy, he said, and I would normally find that empty
but he said it differently

and everything stopped.

I've made a pact to never pay for things I could produce myself
and getting home is one of them.
But my bike was stolen
by these god damn humans
and the bus was crowded
with people
and the tube was filled with them
too
so I took a cab and sat down in the back,
said 'take me home' and stared out the window,
wishing to be left alone,
or left alone in the cab
for a year
at least,
because I like sitting empty in things that take me places.
But the cab driver was of a different kind.
The kind who talks and laughs and sings along to the radio
and he wouldn't shut up.
He told me about the Italian singer on the radio
without me asking
and he sang along and asked if I liked it
and I smiled and tried to give a hint
but he didn't care,
just kept singing and laughing,
and I found it strange because he was a taxi driver,
driving youths all night long
with a photo of his son in the rear view,
but still he sang like the happiest man on earth
and I don't know how
but he made me feel safe like a child

and it was nice.
It was a long drive home and when he helped me out
he said he liked my dress
and I never wear dresses
but it made me feel nice
and so did he
and it was an awful night
but that taxi driver made me feel fine.
Small but okay.

I fell asleep with the dress still on and I still have it on as I sit by my
desk
in the corner
writing words on this paper
to make sense of last night,
and it's strange because it was a sad night,
or could have been,
but now all I think about
or will think about
is that man,
who sang Italian songs
and had a photo of his son,
and said he liked my dress,
and he made me feel like a child again.
He drove me home
and called me 'kid'
and it was nice.

THE YOUTH (OR THE TRUTH)

We are the youth who never cared to settle in
and we were too sure of ourselves to even explain
our actions
and who cares if they get it or not.
we were never here for you, or them, or anyone else
but ourselves
and that's selfish and inconvenient,
because we call ourselves a community,
a new tribe, group, family,
but at the end of the day we care for no one
but ourselves.

I spend my days reading and preaching. Writing manifestos of how
free we could be, mentioning Thoreau and Joseph Campbell, Emerson
and The Stoics, and I speak of teachers and mentors, the great perhaps
and the great divide.
I have flowers in my hair and only eat food I've made myself, because
someone told me about the kids in the third world
with poison in their veins and dreams held fast inside their minds
and I guess someone told them about the first world,
because there was a letter
I got the other week,
from a boy I'm not allowed to mention, and he had written the letter
at night when no one saw because he wasn't allowed to write letters
to people like me,
and he snuck it in the corner of the rucksack of his friend
who had spent two years planning his escape.
He wrote of the government and the Man, the people and the rest
and used words I couldn't understand,
because at night after I think I've done alright

I close the door to my apartment, locks and thick walls,
and I open the windows because I can separate inside and outside
here,
mine and theirs,
and I can eat whatever I want in any way I want
because I'm a grown up now and so I'm free.
Free to be and do and say
and eat
as I please
and on the paper I can call myself educated
because I spent years reading books by people who also call themselves
educated
because they think they know things
because they also read books by people who called themselves
educated because they also read books
but I want to strip the walls, get rid of the middle hands and go
straight to the war.
I don't want to read about people who read about people or watch a
tragedy with six layers of screens and actors, censored words in
between me and the real ground;
I want to be in the dirt. I want to touch their hands and hear the guns
and feel the heat,
or swim in the Walden pond and see the stars myself.
I'm tired of reading my way through experiences and making it up
inside my head and I want ecstasy that feels real and not a vague
hallucination from poison in my lungs.
'Cause I think there is something to be said about the way the youth
smoke pot like it's breakfast because they're tired of familiarity, seeking
strangeness, and there is something to be said about taking the easy
way out.
Escapism.

You can watch or read or seek every corner of the earth through a
screen with the light you wish to have,
but I'm tired of the plastic inorganic bullshit my surroundings are
filled with
and if I was brave enough I'd put this room on fire this very second.
I have wine enough to watch it burn the whole night, observing my
old chains of possessions burn up in flames.
What a beautiful view.
What a beautiful thought.

But I am not
that brave,
so instead I lie here on my very well built bed
on the 3rd floor
in this safe building,
writing about rebels and new-thinkers
as if I was one of them.

Lastly,
there is something to be said about the difference between the thinkers
and the doers. The believers and the achievers. The ones with good
intentions, and the ones who might fail but at least act.
The ones who follow the leader, thinking they're just as good and will
end up wherever it will be good to end up,
and the ones who take the lead and make sure to end up where they
want to end up.

I drink eight cups of coffee a day and buy new books and collect vinyl
made of plastic,
and I am sorry for this bullshit because I wish I didn't.

ADDICTIONS

He told me
"Don't write what you think they want you to write, write about the things that matter." And I said that what matters to them doesn't matter to me and what matters to me doesn't matter to you and he said
"You're overestimating yourself. Underestimating them."
I kept my eyes on the ground and I was ashamed and embarrassed because I've spent the last five years trying to turn myself into an artist and today I admitted to a close enough stranger that I did not know how to be it – an artist – anymore. When people know about it. It is different now. It was different back then. When it was innocent and unread, unheard, and I was unseen, but now you're eating my words like wolves, rearranging and recreating, and
I spent the last five years turning myself into something I did not know the meaning of, and now here I am.
So I said I'm in doubt and he said about what and I said about art.
About writing. Music. Dancing.
For I don't mean to be judged but still I judge
myself
and everyone else
and I wish my art could be taken as it is.
For now when I sit down to write I think of them, and you, and all the rest,
so he said "don't write what you think they want you to write, write about the things that matter." And I said that what matters to them doesn't matter to me and what matters to me doesn't matter to you and he said "you're overestimating yourself. Underestimating them. Underestimating me."

He was quiet and so was I, like I often am when I don't believe what I hear and so he turned around and threw a "try me" over his shoulder. "Write about what matters. To you. Tonight. And try me. See if I care."

So here it goes.

My glass is empty and the pencil is sharp. Windows opened and my head is blurred, and so now I will tell you about what matters, to me.

Addiction.

I'd like to talk about addictions. Because my name is Charlotte Eriksson and I'm an addict. I've been my whole life and I still am and I still will be for the rest of my life

but more lately than ever

because I am controlled by uncontrolled powers

and I am a slave.

Slave to my art. Slave to my mind. Slave to hunger, to poetry, to habits. To voices in my head

telling me to do things

or not do things.

Telling me to doubt

when I want to believe

and believe

when I doubt

and this is what matters

to me.

An addict

wants to stay shallow because their interior is the thing that scares him more than the devil does, because the interior is what makes him an addict in the first place and he knows it, but there's nothing he can do.

He's an addict to his own addiction even, and so whatever you choose
to do about it will force you to start a war against some kind of part in
or on yourself and how do you do that?
When you're tired.
When you're scared.
And small and alone and I didn't eat for 13 days and I call that an
addiction. I run for 160 min every morning and I call that an
addiction. I poured whisky in my coffee every morning for a year and
I call that an addiction.

I was clinging to a person so hard that I did not know how to breathe
when he let go
and I call that an addiction.

I am all or nothing.
I am summer or rain.
Love or hate. Happy or suicidal,
and there's nothing in between here,
nothing mediocre.
It's extraordinary or completely fucking useless
and I never learned the middle.
So I run or I don't run.
I love or I don't love.
I eat or don't eat
and drink
or don't drink
and he told me to write about what matters
and so I will write about what matters,
because I don't think I'm alone here.
I do not think I am alone

for everyone I meet is an addict in one way or another and maybe I'm
just drawn to the wrong people but why do we spend our lives
building those chains
for ourselves
and then wish we were free,
and why do I create those chains
for myself
and then wish I was free,
and how do you do it.
How do you do it.
How do you do this.

EMPTINESS

I don't feel anything. Nothing.
I've tried everything. To trigger me, shock me, start any kind of signal
or sign of aliveness somewhere in my heart
but it's still. Numb. Empty.
I stayed awake for days and slept for days.
I didn't eat and I ate, I didn't run and I ran too long
and I've tried everything.
I feel nothing.

I've read about people who go through things, like life, and I've read
about people who go through hell and back, metaphorically or
literally,
and nothing much gets to them after that. They cease to feel euphoria
and excitement
or heart-staggering pain.
They don't feel the smell of horizons and possibilities the first day of
spring
like I always do,
and they don't see the strugglesome darkness in December. When the
buses are crowded and streets are empty.

I wake up and turn around, go through my limbs like under a
telescope. My feet, legs, arms, heart – they're all there. But I don't feel
them.
I get myself up and out to the people, where it's easier to breathe, for
I'm not as stuck in my own self. But not even the passage of a day
changes things or move things
and I have ceased to feel.
I feel nothing. I am nothing.

I don't feel anything.

JOURNAL II

What I want to know is what you do when you no longer dare to
dream
because dreams turned you down too many times,
or turned you inside out,
from memories still aching like thunder,
and what I want to know is how you go on
when you look around
and don't see anywhere you want to go
without the only person
you can't have.

LETTER FROM A DRUNK

It's Tuesday and I'm back on track.
Sorry, I mean back on the train.
The right train
on the right track.
Up and to the left.
It's August and I've wasted months reading books up and down on
self-development and new starts. Great minds sharing great thoughts
about getting greater than the greats
and I learn while sitting lonely on the floor with another drink,
getting drunk to convince myself of getting great
(when all I really want is an escape),
and so I read all those self help books
to maybe one day start
to get great,
relating all to sober thoughts
for all I read and relate to
is
sober
thoughts
because mine are not,
and have not been
lately,
and I'm young and free and
spiritual,
they say,
so no one really minds.
But they don't see my mind
for if they did they would
mind

for it is cloudy and foggy and there is never a clear thought passing by
anymore. I'm escaping to new lands and streets every morning
but more often than not it is not enough
and so I drink
or smoke
or run
the fog away
and it's accepted in different ways
but in the end it's all the same
and never clears the smoke
anyway.

But people don't want to hear this.
I am young and just a free spirit,
they say,
laughing it off
like it doesn't mean a thing,
and so do I,
but one day I won't,
because I'm chasing escapes and they don't know and I'm not scared
but still wish I was because something tells me I should be.

JOURNAL III

I thought of you and how I thought I would never have to live
without you,
again,
and I was right,
I guess.
I will never live without the thought of you,
never live without the thought of you,
   ever again.

   You'll be forever on my mind.

FROM MY VIEW

I'm circling around the airport, the landing, the finish line. They said we had to stay in the air for five minutes, to wait for the green light. But the minutes turned into an hour and the hour turned into two and the airplane ran out of fuel and now we're running circles around the city I was supposed to land in but never got to settle in. Can we turn around? Get a hotel on the way, a few hours of sleep and then keep going? I ask, but no, we have to stay in the air Miss. We have to keep going.

I used to have a bright vision for the future. Always spring in my head, the grass growing greener. And I never envisioned the rainy days, the dark ones. I was going places and seeing things. Greeting people and achieving things. And I do, I guess, from time to time, from a distance.

From a distance.

I fly in circles above the ground, unable to come down and try to use the time as effectively as I can. I read things and write things and create upon the small blocks of skills I've grown. Looking up from time to time to ask if we can land soon? Or turn back, find a hotel, a bed for the night? To rest. But no, they tell me, you have to keep going Miss, and what else is there to do.

So I stay put, achieving things from a distance where no one can reach or see or touch, me or my things, and some nights I throw a thought to what it would feel like to be down there, around the others. To walk the earth and talk the talk and I wonder what my art would turn into if I let them touch it with their time. Would it turn to gold or turn to dust? Mean more or less or just nothing much?

I am young, they tell me, still time to land and fly and choose another land to match, but still I fly in circles above the people I never got to

meet or see or simply try to be, and I use my time here as effectively as I can.
I use my time up here as effectively as I can.

I hope it looks sweeter from the ground.
I hope my voice sounds better
from the ground.

I WILL NEVER SAY NO

But we don't make use of all these treasures people have shared with us. We know so much about others, but we don't notice, or realize, or simply ignore. Do you even understand the magnificent weight another person trusts you with when he shares a simple statement of what his day was like? His favorite book, what he's listening to when no one knows or a story about that girl he fell secretly in love with five years ago. How he wrote letters every night and then burned them in the shed behind her neighbor's house because he was embarrassed.

If we could only learn to shelter the way another person let us be a part of their world, their life, their being,

and even if it seems like just a little part, such a small thing to be something to care about, we must understand that nothing is little when it comes to a life.

I, for that matter, find it much easier to answer with a made-up name, fictional stories of where I'm going and where I've been, than to actually answer with the truth and my real name. If I just arrived or if I'm on my way. Who I'd like to be and who I might have been yesterday. So when I do, please know I'm giving you a key to something that is mine and mine only, not to be taken lightly: my world—the place where I will spend the rest of my life.

So we must learn to shelter other people and the treasures they sometimes share with us. Like a simple awareness of someone saying 'ok' instead of 'good'.

I will never close my eyes again. I don't want to miss a thing.

I will never say no.

THE FLOWER

It's January and I'm kicking snow off the ground. I just threw out the flower you made me promise to water, handle with care, because I was too careless, you said. Careless with things and people, around me and behind
and I remember being still for just a second or two, thinking that it's so much easier to leave and start anew than take care of what's already here.

I said yes and took the flower home, placed it by my window and made a promise to keep it green and alive, satisfied until the summer no longer bloomed. But life woke up the slumber I'd been inhabiting for so long and all became wonderfully stressful. I went places and saw people, and the flower by the window in my room was never on my mind
and not even as I drew the curtains back and forth as I awoke and said good night did I notice it's slowly resting head.
So now it's January with flowers hidden well under a thick layer of snow, and soon the spring will find its way, the soil will shoot them far off the ground and if there were no more flowers and colors as the spring arrived, wouldn't you miss them? Wouldn't you do anything to let them decorate the ground you rarely notice. Things you never notice until they're not there.
So I'm thinking that I must learn how to take care of the things I have, here, before me, like treasures I somehow managed to find, because I never realize they're treasures until they're gone. Or not there. Like flowers taken for granted in the spring: if no one waters them or give them shelter during the cold, they will simply not grow, or stay
or come back.
Like virtues and feelings, places and
people

73

because see, I have a small amount of people around me with vastly large minds

and I never seem to water them, because life gets in the way. It gets hectic and wonderfully stressful

and I forget to notice them as the seasons come and go

and it's not until the winter comes and I need a warm hand to hold that I turn around to find some kind of embrace

that I realize

I'm alone.

And so I open that door to my cave in the spring, when it suits me just fine, expecting a spectacle of nature and blooming flowers on the ground, waiting for me to have time,

but I never nourished them. Only took for granted, and so that's that.

Learning how to go on fine by yourself is a skill worth mastering, and I've mastered it for years. This year will be the year I learn to go on not by myself

and I will learn to water the plants I'm given

if I so have to ink it on my skin

and experiences can hurt but god they teach us and I am up for the challenge.

Today I bought a new flower, picked it out with my own heart, and as I placed it by the window with the snow and the cold and the frost outside,

I made a silent promise

to keep it warm.

JOURNAL IIII

I am not sad anymore.
I am not weak or tender or quiet like you remember because the
second you said those words and closed that door, I sold my soul to
the part of myself I had buried in order to love you, to let you touch
every inch of my rotten body, for I wanted to be touchable and not so
strange. Not so sad and tender, like I've always been, they say, so I
changed.
And then your glances and words throwing knives with no return
about my change of habits and ways of living, being, and I nodded
and smiled, dying silently a little bit inside.

But I am not sad anymore,
and if you could see me now you wouldn't be so awfully tall for I've
grown both inner and outer and I can run for hours; I've taught my
muscles to carry this weight you left me with because I was constantly
struggling with being weightless and heavy,
sad and angry,
in love and unloved.

Know that if I cry,
it's not out of sadness.
It's because I spent a year on you I can't get back
and it was the best year of my life
because I learned something I could never learn alone:
I don't need anyone else to make myself grow.

Are you in love? What makes your heart beat faster?
What do you want people to think about
when they hear your name?

———————

"Pause you who read this, and think for a moment of the long chain of iron or gold, of thorns or flowers, that would never have bound you, but for the formation of the first link on one memorable day."
— *Charles Dickens, Great Expectations*

I AM SORRY

To the girl at the table by the window.
I am sorry. I am so sorry.
I saw you sink deeper in your chair with every word he spoke, though
they seemed few, and I saw you grasp your own elbows, clasping tight
until your knuckles got white.
I am sorry. I am so sorry.
I am sorry for the night ahead of you. You will replay every
conversation and find better things you could have said, should have
said. You will search for small clues of a storm, just some kind of sign.
You should have noticed that things were not right.
You will walk many streets without remembering the way, for your
head is on the ground, or in the sky, and you will forget simple things,
like showering, eating, checking emails, how to sleep.
You will stay on the right side of the bed
and when you finally manage to fall asleep again, you will wake up by
trying to take his hand
but not finding one,
and things will hit you like a gun shot in your chest
over and over again
and I am sorry. I am so sorry.

To the man at the table by the window.
I am sorry. I am so sorry.
I saw you tackle your way through the labyrinth of words you'd built
up
and I saw you sit on your hands, as if not to let them take hers and
hold her
like you've done so many times.
And I saw your eyes slowly turning blank but trying to stay sharp,

for you had made a decision after all, though you doubted it now, and things had to be done.

There are seasons for blooming

and seasons for going

and you can not stay if you want to keep moving and

I am sorry. I am so sorry.

I am sorry for the night ahead of you, when you will replay every single word you said and wonder if you could have said it in any other way. Chose your words more carefully, made the gun shot a bit softer.

You will replay the holiday last year, when you were still in love, and her smile made every other grey in comparison.

You will see her drink her coffee in the morning, by the table in the sun, and recall her smell when you kissed her.

Close enough to hear her heart beat, like you did so many times

but never enough

and you will wonder if things could have been saved. Changed and savored, and maybe you're the weak one, for giving up.

To the couple walking separate ways from the table by the window.
I am sorry. I am so sorry.

I saw you both run through the past five years in your minds, and I saw you both gasping for air at the thought of another five years, in this world, without each other,

for you had it all planned out once. Not materialistic or physical, but together. As long as you had each other you would go on well.

But I observed you from the other side, sitting by the same table by the same window for months in a row, and the seasons changed from green to grey

and so did you

and I'm not sure where the switch turned black but the novels I wrote about a couple by a window, throwing kisses by just eyes, turned into lies I could no longer write

and it took me months to see the truth in the elegy you'd turned into,
and I think it did
for you too,
and now I feel like a liar writing wills though I'm not dying,
for this is not the end. It is rather the beginning.
Because seasons come and go, bloom and leave behind and so do we
and now you
and you experienced each other, to the fullest, I hope, and it doesn't
have to be sad. Doesn't have to be lonely. But still:
I am sorry. I am so sorry.
I am sorry for how he slowly stood up, insecure like he'd never felt
before,
and how she did not know if she should stand up too, or stay, or how
she could do anything at all
for her limbs got weak
and his hands were shaking as he put one on her shoulder, not
knowing how close he could get,
now,
and I am sorry. I am so sorry.

To whoever you are, a year from now.
I am sitting on a train, an early Wednesday in August. The sun is
rising over the rails and I'm on my way. A new town, a new phase. I
bought many suitcases and colored my hair in every color I could find.
Found new friends and new homes, introduced myself with different
names every time, but still as I shut the door at night, I was no one
but me.

You will dream about him for months, but that is not the sad part in
this story. The sad part is how it never matched up with what really
was, when it was, for we always romanticize the things that no longer
are, and it's about the sadness in how we never miss what we have, but

only what we don't have, and missing always conquer any other feeling.
Like love,
while it blooms,
and I am sorry. I am so sorry.
I am sorry for not knowing how to move on and let go when I am fully aware of how nothing ever stays the same, and it shouldn't, for life is the constant flow, the ebb and low, and so I am sorry.
I am sorry for not knowing how to say this better or in any other way than
 it simply will get better.
You will get better.
He will
and she will
and it might take time
but there will be an early morning in August when you find yourself on yet another train, towards a new place, a new plan, and you realize that you did not think about him this morning, waking up. And she was not beside you while making coffee, in your mind. And you wish her well, and hope he is happy, and you will send her a thought now and then, and maybe if you see him on the street in a year from now you will not be sad or angry or hurt. Just happy, that he still is, and that you still are, and it's the way life blooms, the ebbs and lows, and it will get better. You will go on well.
It will take time,
but you will go on well.

THE RHYTHM OF THE SEA

(I will find comfort in the rhythm of the sea. The fluidity of constant change,
moving certain like the proudest wave.)

I've been shifting weight lately, left to right, pros and cons, this or that. I've been stubborn enough to get to try out many different ways of living. Many different ways of being. I've tried several versions of myself, both inwardly and outwardly. Identity crisis, some call it, or insecurity. And maybe they're right, I guess, but I never saw myself as way too lost because I believe in the endless possibilities of oneself and that's why I flow. The certainty in constant change.

Building safety and comfort is hard and takes time – if you want it to last. It's easy to throw a house up on common ground and plant your seeds. Grow your roots and make the decision that this will be called my home from now on.
Building a home is easy when you build it on external things, like the ground of a place, a house, a city, a person. But building a home in and of itself, that can't be burnt to the ground, raptured or simply taken away, is hard. I might take the long way home but my first and biggest decision when I closed that door to my childhood room a few years ago was to build my safety and home in and of myself, never in a place, and that's why I flow.
x xx   certain, like the rhythm of a wave

It might take me a life time and it might cause me more worrying and sadness than actual strength, but I will be chasing a home in myself for the rest of my life, if I so have to walk homeless at the bottom of the sea to get there. This is my decision to refuse to learn or find comfort in material belongings or safe social net lines.

See, my aim is not to survive

but to be thrown to the wolves with adrenaline still pumping in my veins and hear the gods laughing saying "that was one hell of a youth" and everything I do I do in order to push my senses and levels of natural ecstasy. I want to be so awake that I pass out by exhaustion every night with a smile on my face and no thoughts of tomorrow because today was all I could ever make of it

and I am sick and tired of boredom. Bored people slumbering boring words about bored habits

and I want to get out.

So this is why I flow. Staying fluid, certain like the sea.

I want to learn how to speak to anyone at any time and make us both feel a little bit better, lighter, richer, with no commitments of ever meeting again. I want to learn how to stand wherever with whoever and still feel stable. I want to learn how to unlock the locks to our minds, my mind, so that when I hear opinions or views that don't match up with mine, I can still listen and understand. I want to burn up lifeless habits of following maps and to-do lists, concentrated liquids to burn my mind and throat

and I want to go back to a natural state of me; to be; to flow. I want to learn to go on well with whatever I have in my hands at the moment with a clear mind

and this is why I flow. The constant flow of life, the way it always pulls me back.

I need to corrupt the patterns I've built in and around myself, stop numbing me out to simply get through the day

and I need to escape the way my humanness constantly finds the easiest way around

and I need to push myself out of a rhythm that makes my heart beat in industrial ways

because I don't want to be afraid of life or living
or hurting or growing.

I am finding my way back to the rhythm of the sea,
to find comfort in the certainty of constant change.

YOU'RE NOT ALONE,

YOU JUST HAVE TO FIND ME.

I've always had this strange sense of 'feeling at home' when I find a song or a band, a poem or a writer that I connect to in some way. Like something in my being says "Oh there you are! I didn't know you were missing but now I feel the void you've filled!" You feel a connection between you and this writer. It's something so mysteriously great about finding a writer or a band that makes you feel like you know each other. Like you get each other, understand each other. And it doesn't matter that you've never met because just knowing that if you did meet, he'd understand, and that makes you feel more familiar. Not so strange. Not so foreign.

Family is a strong word with many meanings, and even though I believe that your biological family is the most important thing you have (if you get along), there's something else behind that word that means more to me.

Family to me means belonging, means understanding and being 'of the same kind.' I've always felt a bit out of place around the people I was supposed to feel at home around, and so I've learned to find that family in others. In people I connect with in a different way than through blood. Like when I find a new writer or singer, they become my family, in a way. I read their words like conversations between them and my most honest state. They make me admit, feel and accept things that my 'real' friends and family never could. So these writers become my family. And isn't that what we're all searching for? Isn't that why music is such a beautiful world, because through it we can find our real spiritual family? The sisters, uncles, and brothers we somehow got separated from at birth. The family you were somehow abducted from at birth, and now you're finding them again, one by one, in this world where you feel like you belong. The world of music, or writing, or photography, or whatever it is you've discovered that makes you so excited or 'in the moment' that you completely forget about the things you're supposed to be or do or learn.

A while ago I stumbled upon an interview with the wonderful writer Gregory Orr, and he put it in words so beautifully. He was saying in the interview that "As a young poet, reading is a search for your lost family. You're looking for your secret poetry fathers and your secret poetry mothers. And cousins and sisters, people who are like you. Not your biological family, but your imaginative family. The family you'd like to be reborn into.

Every time you've found a poet you absolutely love, you've found another relative. People who are spiritual relatives. And that means you're not alone. It means that you read Walt Whitman and you feel that recognition and think 'My God! This is my strange great uncle Walt!' It makes it easier for you to live. To know that you're not alone. And so these poems become a part of your life."

By now I've been lucky enough to find and build a beautiful little family that I feel a part of. With writers and songwriters that I've never met, but also with YOU. You who listen to my music or read my writings and can understand, in my or your own way, and if you can find something to like or understand or keep in these very words, I am happy I have met you. You get it, get me, and that gives me the same sense of family even though it's in reverse. You found me, or I found you. Or maybe, rather, we found each other because of something that is deeper than the town you grew up in, or the school you went to, or the people you happened to hang out with once. We found each other because we are touched by something, together.

I think this is why I always will go back to music and art to find comfort, because I know that at any moment wherever I am, no matter how alone I feel or how tired or misunderstood I am, there is always someone out there who knows this song, or this poem, or this book or myth or feeling, and they get it too. They're with me.

If you find your family through something deeper than blood or material belongings, social rank or which school you go to, you've found a family that is stronger than anything.

So thank you for finding me. Thank you for letting me find you.
    Thank you
        for being you.

IT COULD HAVE BEEN SO BEAUTIFUL

It could have been so beautiful.
The way I was too young for my age to run away
but still did
because memories killed me like flashbacks,
shot straight in the dark
every night I passed that spot
on that street
like that night,
remembered so god damn well.
and it was disgusting and ugly,
his hands where they just should have not
been
but still,
it could have been so beautiful,
because it made me who I am.
Makes me who I am.

It could have been so beautiful.
The way our elbows always collide and not a single word was needed
to make each other laugh. I laughed at your existence, I said, and you
laughed even harder and that's how we spent our time.
It could have been so beautiful,
the way the first hit felt good and something to deserve
because I've read every psychology book you can find on human
behavior and know for a fact that anger grows from caring
too much
and so it was a privilege to be in the war zone with someone like you.
How much you must have cared to hit that well
and that hard

and I remember saying thank you
and I'm sorry
at the same time
because what else is there to say.

It could have been so beautiful.
The way I learned and got free and swore to never love another person
ever again
and it could have been so beautiful
the way I actually did.
But winter came too soon
and I grew smaller and we grew colder
and "I love you" got thrown around like habits
too rooted to give a damn
and it took a year
they say
for me to rid myself from habits rooted too deeply
and well
and still:
it could have been so beautiful.

There was a flower a found in the church after my grand mother's
funeral
this time
last year
and I took and kept it
like a treasure hidden well.
I did not know why I stole it
and why I saw it or meant to keep it
but so I did
and now it's August and I find myself sitting in a foreign land
again

drunk from too many thoughts and dreams
and memories hidden well
and there are certain moments when I can slowly work it out together.
Like dot to dot, tracing patterns on a map,
and it all makes sense but still absolutely not
because things could have been so beautiful
but just ended up being
not
but still
they are,
because listen:

I am young and lost and know nothing about pain or love or anything
in between
but what I do know is that I've seen things
I don't wish for others to see,
and I've felt things
I don't wish for others to feel,
and still I sit alive in a foreign city
thinking about someone,
wishing that the someone was here
and if there's anything others have taught me it is that I don't need
them to make myself feel okay
but still I think of him
and his hands
and how he says my name
and that's all I need
to know that
I will be okay, after all.
I will be okay, in spite of it all.
See, ugliness is a fact
but beauty is a virtue

and I've seen it.
I see it
and know it
and will try to keep it
treasured like a secret at the bottom of the sea,
bottled up not to be taken for granted,
like
his hand in mine.

like his hand
in mine.

In spite of it all,
I am okay.

DRIFTED

Sometimes you find yourself drifted up on dry land after capsizing somewhere out there, far out at sea. You threw yourself out into the unknown and it was exciting. He had magic in his eyes and spoke words of warmth and safety; his smell felt like home.

But the storm was too dark and strong and the boat cracked and somewhere along the way he drifted further out and you used the small power you had left to swim, to save yourself, to sip air into your collapsed lungs.

The waves led you up on land and you ignored the days coming and going, until one morning, you finally opened your eyes. The still lightness from the sun rising out there, the waves making their way to wash away the dirt from your bones, and not much feels wrong, or right, or anything at all. Your body found a beautiful rest by the water's edge and the wreck of the love you once knew is gone and so you stand up and simply keep soldiering on.

There are times when you use every cell of your heart to love someone or something or anything at all, and when that strength is used up, or ignored, nothing much bothers you.

Nothing much bothered you for a while and you kept walking like a silhouette through this town, saying hi's and goodbyes, acting polite at all times. But there is no fire in your heart; you are not very concerned.

There are times when you find yourself drenched and dehydrated, undernourished in all kinds of ways, and you become a house where the wind blows straight through, because no one bothers the crack in the window or lock on the door, and you're the house where people come and go as they please, because you're simply too unimpressed to care. You let people in who you really shouldn't let in, and you let them walk around for a while, use your bed and use your books, and await the day when they simply get bored and leave. You're still not bothered, though you knew they shouldn't have been let in in the first place, but still you just sit there, apathetic like a beggar in the desert.

There are also beautiful people passing through, who actually knock on the door, even though it's wide open, and they walk in carefully, asking things like "can I help?" and "are you okay?" and it's nice. It feels warm and there are seconds when you think you feel your heart beat again.
But you're still tired, and even though you want to make the good ones stay, scream "help!" and "can you stay?", you're just too drenched. Tired. Tired. Tired. Just a wreck from the love and the ship that went wrong and the door is still open and you're a house where the wind blows straight through and it's getting colder so they leave. They leave you left alone and you sit there for a long time with new people coming in and walking away and for a while you just get by and you're not concerned.

There are times when we're just simply too tired to be happy, to get back up on our feet. You have been there, or will be there, or maybe are there, watching clouds from the ground right now, and I am here to tell you that you are still doing okay. Those times are not to be feared, nothing to avoid, and watching the clouds drift and come and go for a while is called healing; that is what our bodies were made for.

There is a pleasure in the off switch. There is a pleasure in the passive living, and one day you will wake up from actually having slept for once, and you will notice the sun again. You will find yourself laughing and smiling and thinking things like "how wonderful!". You will go out on the streets by yourself and enjoy the simple pleasure of your own company, and you will feel just fine, even though you can't see it now.

It is okay to turn away from the world from time to time, just to find a new place in it where you can build a new home, new comforts, new beginnings, and there is a pleasure in the off switch.

No matter where you are—on your feet, in the sky, or on the ground watching clouds drift off and come and go—you're in the right place. Doing the right thing at the right time.

There is a plan for you.

You're doing just fine.

"She is all the great heroines of the world in one. She is more than an individual. I love her, and I must make her love me. I want to make Romeo jealous. I want the dead lovers of the world to hear our laughter, and grow sad. I want a breath of our passion to stir dust into consciousness, to wake their ashes into pain. "
— Oscar Wilde, *The Picture of Dorian Gray*

ABOUT THE AUTHOR

Charlotte Eriksson is a songwriter and author from Sweden, currently living somewhere in Europe, wherever the music plays at the moment. She left everything she had and knew as a teenager, and moved to England to create a life for herself that made her excited to wake up in the morning. Since then she has started her own artist collective *Broken Glass Records*, written four books (*Empty Roads & Broken Bottles; in search for The Great Perhaps, Another Vagabond Lost To Love, You're Doing Just Fine, Everything changed when I forgave myself*, and *He loved me some days. I'm sure he did.*), and released 4 LPs under the artist name The Glass Child. Her writings have been published on sites like Thought Catalog, Bella Grace Magazine and Rebelle Society.

AUTHOR NOTE

As a small independent author, I write books for the pure fulfillment of connecting with souls out there, who might be like me. Who might recognize themselves in my story. The thought that my words might mean something to someone out there is what keeps me going during my dark days. If you have found any joy or comfort in my words, please don't be shy ... Say hi to me online, send me a picture of you and this book, tag me on instagram, or tell me about a memory you'll never forget. If you want to help me tell the world about my books and story, it would mean the whole universe if you wanted to write a few nice words about this book as a review on Amazon & Goodreads. Tell all your friends and family about it. Share your favorite quote from the book on instagram, tumblr, twitter ... Tag me so I can find you! But most of all, go out and take your place in the world, for only you can fill it. Together we can make the world a softer place.

Because I love you …

Because I love you (and because by reading this book and my words, you've held my heart in your hand) I have a little gift prepared for you.
If you go to: www.CharlotteEriksson.com/free-ebook
you can download my 2nd book
Another Vagabond Lost To Love
for free, straight to your email right away.
I hope you will like it

I have written four other books called
Another Vagabond Lost To Love: Berlin Stories
Empty Roads & Broken Bottles; in search for The Great Perhaps
Everything Changed When I Forgave Myself
He loved me some days. I'm sure he did.
You can read all about them on my website
www.CharlotteEriksson.com
There you will also find excerpts, quotes and pictures of the books.

www.instagram.com/justaglasschild
contact@charlotteeriksson.com

You can purchase signed copies of all my books,
signed CDs + apparel in my online store:
www.CharlotteEriksson.com/shop

"Suffering has been stronger than all other teaching, and has taught me to understand what your heart used to be. I have been bent and broken, but - I hope - into a better shape."
— Charles Dickens, Great Expectations

Poems

Made in the USA
Columbia, SC
30 September 2023